Natural Antiaging Herbs

Author

Dr Abdul Razzaque Nohri

Researcher and Writer

Contributor

Bill Soukup

Owner @Antiagingextracts

Copyright © 2020 Abdul Razzaque

All rights reserved.

DEDICATION

This book is dedicated to all acid victims round the globe.

Preface

No one likes to have wrinkles, saggy skin and age spots and tired complexions. As we age our skin starts to show these signs. We need to deal with these signs very wisely and gently.

The aging process begins as we born. There are two different types of changes that occur in the skin.

<u>Chronological Aging Changes</u> occur in the skin resulting from the passage of time as we age and thus these changes cannot be controlled. However, these changes can be reduced or slow down by using natural herb extracts. Clinical manifestation of chronologically aged skin includes xerosis, laxity, wrinkles, slackness, and the appearance of a variety of benign neoplasms such as seborrheic keratosis and cherry angioma. Hair becomes depigmented, terminal hair are converted to vellus hair and overall loss of hair is increased. There are also changes in nail plate.

<u>2. Photo Aging Changes</u> These changes result from chronic sun exposure. Some of the plant extracts like dill seed extract have the ability to scavenge free radicals, to protect the skin matrix through the inhibition of enzymatic degradation, or to promote collagen and or elastin synthesis in the skin. Certainly, there is a place for herbal principles in antiaging extracts.

The one and only solution to deal is the use of pure Natural anti-aging products. Because most market products appear to be packed with man-made chemicals that have the potential to irritate, both us and our environment.

Our skin quality deteriorates when the molecules within our skin cells are attacked by free radicals and left in a damaged state. Free radicals are unstable molecules in our environment and can be caused by, for example, pollution, cigarette smoke and herbicides. Exposure to ultraviolet light from sunlight causes immense damage alone, with some reports suggesting it causes up to 90% of the symptoms of premature ageing (aging before time).

Table of Contents

Ideal Natural Anti-Aging Preparation

First of all, let's understand our skin in a very simple way.

Our skin has three layers: the epidermis, the dermis and the subcutaneous tissue. The epidermis is the outer most layer, and it thins with age. The dermis provides the structural support, or springiness, via collagen and elastin fibres, and these get tired and wear out with age. The subcutaneous tissue provides the fat cells that keep our faces plump. We lose these cells as we age, and so our faces sag. It all conspires together to create wrinkles.

No one likes to have wrinkles, saggy skin and age spots and tired complexions. As we age our skin starts to show these signs. We need to deal with these signs very wisely and gently.

The one and only solution to deal is the use of pure Natural anti-aging products. Because most market products appear to be packed with man-made chemicals that have the potential to irritate, both us and our environment.

Our skin quality deteriorates when the molecules within our skin cells are attacked by free radicals and left in a damaged state. Free radicals are unstable molecules in our environment and can be caused by, for example, pollution, cigarette smoke and herbicides. Exposure to ultraviolet light from sunlight causes immense damage alone, with some reports suggesting it causes up to 90% of the symptoms of premature ageing (aging before time).

An attacked skin molecule can itself become a free radical, thus triggering a chain reaction that can lead to the destruction of the entire skin cell. The older we are the freer radicals we accumulate. Anti-oxidants are the enemy of free radicals, and our bodies produce them naturally. They 'neutralise' or repair free radicals and break the chain reaction that eventually causes skin cells to break down. Before the age of 30 our bodies produce enough anti-oxidants to be able to cope with the onslaught of free radicals. After that, we could do with a bit of help. And of course, if you want to keep chemical nasties away from your skin a natural anti-aging product is the best option.

Advantages Of Natural Anti-Aging Products Over Modern Cosmetics

Natural anti-aging products are only the ideal solution to deal. The pros of natural anti-aging over chemical made cosmetics are outlined as under.

- They work in two ways, either they stop the destruction of elastin and collagen or they help in the increased production of both essential skin care proteins. Elastin and collagens are the major proteins responsible for maintaining the structure and elasticity of skin as well as keeping skin firm and supple. Both proteins decrease with age, leading to the shrinkage and wrinkles of the skin. The natural anti-aging products contain the ingredients which are anti-oxidants, which stop the production of free radicals that leads to the stoppage of destruction of elastin and collagen.
- They are manufactured without alcohol, which causes the denaturation of active ingredients of product. Denaturation is a process in which essential ingredients of a product are destroyed by alcohol.
- They are produced without excess heat, because heat destroy the natural constituents of preparations. There is a particular acceptable limit of heat beyond which ingredients are destroyed.
- The ingredients are purely natural so there is no chance of adverse effects as with traditional cosmetics. Purely natural and semisynthetic ingredients produce no any harm/side

effect while the synthetic/pure chemical ingredients have more potential to produce adverse effects.

- They contain multiple ingredients which have proven efficacy for skin care and all the problems associated with skin. Ingredients include vitamins (specially vitamin C, E, A, K, B3, B5 and choline), anti-oxidants (like Co-Enzyme Q10, Flavonoids, Niacinamide, Polyphenols etc), collagen, elastin, amino acids, proteins, peptides etc.
- They don't contain any harmful preservative such as organic acids unlike modern cosmetics.
- Natural anti-aging products contain multiple ingredients rather than single ingredient. Different natural ingredients such as vitamins, proteins, amino acids, peptides give an ultra-strength to the preparation to show outstanding effects unlike using single ingredients.
- They are non-toxic, non-irritants, non-comedogenic and non-reactive to skin.

Skin Care Benefits of Dill Seed

The aging process begins as we born. There are two different types of changes that occur in the skin.

1.Chronological Aging Changes These changes occur in the skin resulting from the passage of time as we age and thus these changes cannot be controlled. However, these changes can be reduced or slow down by using natural herb extracts. Clinical manifestation of chronologically aged skin includes xerosis, laxity, wrinkles, slackness, and the appearance of a variety of benign neoplasms such as seborrheic keratosis and cherry angioma. Hair becomes depigmented, terminal hair are converted to vellus hair and overall loss of hair is increased. There are also changes in nail plate.

2. Photo Aging Changes These changes result from chronic sun exposure.

Some of the plant extracts like dill seed extract have the ability to scavenge free radicals, to protect the skin matrix through the inhibition of enzymatic degradation, or to promote collagen and or elastin synthesis in the skin. Certainly, there is a place for herbal principles in antiaging extracts.

Dill *(Peucedanum graveolens)* is a member of the Apiaceae family and is native to the Mediterranean and Black Sea regions. Dill seed oil is produced mainly in Europe. For aromatherapy purposes, it is well combined with mint, nutmeg, other spicy oils and citrus oils. Following are the different ways and studies that has proved the potency and effectiveness of Dill seed extract in anti-aging process.

1. Dill seed extract stimulates elastin synthesis by activating dermal fibroblasts, as per study conducted in 2006 in Experimental Dermatology.

2. The dill seed extract also increases the production of the elastin precursor, tropo-elastin. The tropo-elastin molecules come together to create elastin.

3. Dermatologist Paul Begoun explains that dill seed has the special ability to attack elastin, "It seems that dill extract helps increase the expression of an enzyme in the skin that generates elastin and helps rebuild the structural integrity of the skin".

4. Dill seed extract contains a biomolecule that stimulates the expression of an enzyme (LOXL) which is an extracellular enzyme that catalyses the cross-linking between microfibrils and tropo-elastin, thereby ensuring elastic fibre functionality. With ageing, LOXL expression decreases, thus participating in the loss of skin elasticity. While Dill seed increases the production and stimulation of LOXL.

5. Fortunately, dill seed is super affordable. Alternatively, we can combine dill seed extract with any of our favourite essential oils safe for the skin to have emollient effects.

6. Dill can be one of the few plants extracts whose Anti-aging properties increase the production of elastin or decrease its destruction with aging.

7. Treatment with the Dill extract promotes the skin elasticity, causes smoothening of wrinkles and face appears remodelled.

Skin Care Benefits of Hesperidin

Three of the better-known bioflavonoids, quercetin, hesperidin, and rutin, have solid research behind them proving their power to prevent and reverse wrinkles, reduce the appearance of age spots, and even fight spider veins and varicose veins. As potent as these plant metabolites are on their own, they exhibit an even greater effect when they're used together, as studies have shown they work synergistically by harmonizing with each other. Together, these three natural ingredients provide the rejuvenating power we need to help redefine aging skin and to fight the signs of premature aging such as spider veins, wrinkles, age spots, and more. Hesperidin is a bioflavonoid, a type of plant pigment with antioxidant and anti-inflammatory effects found primarily in unripe citrus fruit. Oranges, grapefruit, lemon, and tangerines contain hesperidin, and it is also available in supplement form. Hesperidin has a similar structure to hydroquinone, a compound that has long been considered the professional gold standard for the treatment of age spots and other hyperpigmentation disorders. Like hydroquinone, hesperidin works by limiting the capacity of the skin cells to produce tyrosinase, the enzyme responsible for producing the skin pigment melanin. However, unlike hydroquinone, hesperidin does not come with a list of side effects. In fact, research has demonstrated that hesperidin safely produces a reduction in tyrosinase activity. By interfering with tyrosinase activity, hesperidin is ultimately able to inhibit the development of age spots. Hesperidin has outstanding potential for cosmetic use. It's vasoprotective and skin-lightening actions work to counteract many of the visible signs of aging. By nourishing and protecting the skin's ability to heal and reproduce, bioflavonoids like quercetin, hesperidin, and rutin help to safely and naturally restore and maintain a more youthful appearance.

Skin Care Benefits of Evening Primrose

Evening Primrose Oil soothes and moisturizes the skin, scalp, and hair while enhancing elasticity. Furthermore, it promotes a healthy, clear, rejuvenated complexion with enhanced radiance and addresses roughness, wrinkles, redness, dryness, and irritation. It facilitates the healing process, reduces the appearance of scars, and calms inflammation. The main chemical constituents of Evening Primrose Oil are: Linoleic Acids (Omega-6), γ-Linolenic Acid (Omega-6), Oleic Acid (Omega-9), Palmitic Acid, and Stearic Acid. Linoleic Acids (Omega-6) are known to moisturize hair and promote its growth, soothe acne and reduce chances of future outbreaks, promote moisture retention in skin and hair and Help slow the look of aging by sustaining skin elasticity and softness. Gamma-Linolenic Acid (Omega-6) is known to nourishes the skin with essential fatty acids and supports the growth of healthier and stronger skin, hair, and nails. Oleic Acids (Omega-9) are known to maintain the softness, suppleness, and radiance of skin and hair, stimulate the growth of thicker, longer, and stronger hair, reduce the appearance of aging, such as premature wrinkles and fine lines, and eliminate dandruff and thereby support hair growth. Palmitic Acid is known to Have emollient properties, soften hair without leaving a greasy or sticky residue. Stearic Acid is known to Have cleansing properties that eliminate dirt, sweat, and excess sebum from hair and skin, Condition and protect hair from damage without diminishing luster or making it feel heavy and Soften skin. Studies have indicated that using evening primrose oil topically might help with hair loss. One **study**, by the University of Maryland, which gave patients who had experienced significant hair loss, primrose oil to take for seven months, found that the patients had significant hair regrowth by the end. "To get even more benefit, mix evening primrose oil with rosemary essential oil, which has also shown to help with hair loss and increase hair thickness," says van Uitert. "Combine several drops of each oil with coconut oil and apply to the area of concern daily." One study, published by the peer-reviewed journal, *Evidence-Based Complementary and Alternative Medicine*, even linked primrose oil to helping with nerve-crush injuries. "At the end of the studies, the injured rats showed significant improvement with nerve damage, and their reflexes were nearly identical to the healthy cohort," van Uitert explains. "The potent level of antioxidants in evening primrose helps to neutralize free radicals, which protect the skin from oxidation in living tissue," explains June Jacobs, CEO of the June Jacobs Spa Collection. "The inclusion of this nourishing ingredient in skin care is known to help with smoothing roughness, too." Baron recommends applying evening primrose oil to your face and neck regularly and even taking primrose supplements twice a day for flawless, youthful looking skin. Evening primrose oil might help relieve symptoms of notoriously difficult-to-treat and painful skin conditions, such as psoriasis and eczema. According to Maat van Uitert, essential oil expert and founder of FrugalChicken, the high omega-6 fatty acid content of primrose oil helps ease symptoms.

Skin Care Benefits of Marshmallow Leaf

There is no any possible research is available regarding the skincare benefits of Marshmallow leaf. However, Marshmallow root has significant health benefits including skin care.

Marshmallow root soothes the nerve-sense system of the skin, which, in turn, reduces skin irritation. The root can also be used topically to treat wounds, burns, insect bites, dry or chapped skin, and even peeling skin. The mucilage properties of the root soften the skin, which is one reason it is an active ingredient in most skin care products. The anti-inflammatory properties of marshmallow root are also helpful in treating eczema. The polysaccharides in the root moisturize the skin and add a protective layer to ultra-sensitive skin. The mucilage in marshmallow root may benefit your hair. It binds with hair proteins and makes the strands appear thicker. This mucilage may also be used as a hair detangle and conditioner.

Skin Care Benefits of Feverfew

Feverfew has uses in folklore medicine for centuries as an herbal treatment for fever and headache, topical skin care products to reduce the appearance of facial redness and skin irritation. Purified Feverfew Extract delivers high antioxidant and anti-irritant benefits. When applied topically, these formulations significantly reduce the appearance of redness and irritation. It has been used to diminish freckles, skin discoloration, and brown spots. Skin Care products use Feverfew in balancing oil free skin because it is anti-inflammatory, healing, skin softening and a perfect ingredient for sensitive skin. It would also be a desirable ingredient for douches, in toners for dry or sensitive skin, for facial steams for sensitive skin, or as an added herb to a bath.

One challenge associated with the topical application of feverfew derivatives is the risk of parthenium dermatitis, a common allergic reaction to plants.

Skin Care Benefits of Alfalfa

Alfalfa has a long history of use in Ayurvedic medicine to treat conditions caused by inflammation and oxidative damage. This is because alfalfa was thought to act as a powerful antioxidant, preventing damage caused by free radicals. Several animal studies have now confirmed its antioxidant effects. Studies found that alfalfa has the ability to reduce cell death and DNA damage caused by free radicals. It does this by both lowering the production of free radicals and improving the body's ability to fight them. One study in mice even found that treatment with alfalfa could help reduce the damage caused by stroke or brain injury. By taking alfalfa supplements or incorporating alfalfa sprouts into your diet, you could be ensuring that your body has what it needs to produce healthy cells for your hair and body. Alfalfa contains high levels of antioxidants, like most herbs. Antioxidants fight the environmental factors that can make hair and skin cells look prematurely aged. This is known as oxidative stress. Using alfalfa for hair could disrupt the oxidative stress on hair cells and restore a glossy, youthful look.

Topical chlorophyll may work as an anti-aging remedy. A study found that applying a gel containing chlorophyllin to the skin reduced signs of photoaging, which is aging that results from sun exposure. The study used skin samples from four healthy women and lasted for 12 days. The results of the study showed that skin treated with chlorophyllin improved in a similar way to skin treated with tretinoin, which is a prescription skin cream that has

been proven to help with skin aging. The authors suggest that using a combination of chlorophyllin and tretinoin could be an effective treatment for reversing the signs of photoaged skin.
Side effects of alfalfa include sun sensitivity and lack of red cells, white cells, and platelets in the blood (from ground alfalfa seeds).

Skin Care Benefits of Spinach

Spinach is a wonderful source of iron, folate, chlorophyll, Vitamin E, magnesium, Vitamin A, fiber, plant protein, and Vitamin C. Due to their antioxidant abilities, Vitamins C, E, and A are especially great for your skin. These antioxidants fight against all types of skin problems. Spinach is a healthy green vegetable that's loaded with beneficial nutrients like folate, iron, and vitamins A and C, all of which may promote hair growth. Vitamin A helps the skin glands produce sebum. This oily substance helps moisturize the scalp to keep hair healthy. Spinach is also a great plant-based source of iron, which is essential for hair growth. Iron helps red blood cells carry oxygen throughout the body to fuel your metabolism and aid growth and repair. Spinach helps clear impurities from the body, which can encourage breakouts. Spinach is rich in chlorophyll which helps cleanse bacteria and toxins from the digestive tract and blood stream. Spinach is rich in Vitamin A, which naturally acts as an anti-acne agent. Spinach is loaded with tons of antioxidants that destroy free radicals in your body. These free radicals damage your skin, thereby causing pre-mature ageing. Thus, eating spinach regularly will maintain the youthfulness of your skin and slow down age-related degeneration, making your skin look younger and rejuvenated.

Skin Care Benefits of Nettle

Nettle is anti-inflammatory, astringent, bactericidal, healing, mildly deodorant and stimulating. It is high in phenols, which give nettle powerful antioxidant properties and help keep the free radicals under control when used in skincare. Research has also found high anti-microbial activity in nettle extracts (Gülçin, 2004). Nettles have been used in skincare remedies for a long time. In an article from 1854, a Dr. Joseph Buller describes replacing the use of liquor arsenicalis (essentially a poisonous 'medicine' used in the 1800s to 'cure' all sorts of ailments) with nettle decoction or extract. Virtually all of his patients were cured of their chronic skin diseases, despite the fact that – in his words – this knowledge was passed down by *"the class of peasantry usually termed 'old women "*. Nettle extract is also used in the treatment of scalp problems and incorporated into a variety of hair products. Nettle roots are used to relieve eczema and dandruff and are reputed to stimulate hair growth. Today, nettle root extract is commonly found as a component of many shampoos and conditioners. Because of its nourishing, diuretic and anti-inflammatory properties, nettle tea is a natural beautifier to skin and hair. It has been shown to clear acne and eczema as well as encourage thicker, shinier hair and new hair growth.

Skin Care Benefits of Licorice Root

Licorice root refers to the dried, unpeeled roots of Glycyrrhiza glabra, containing not less than 4 percent glycyrrhizic acid and 25 percent water-soluble matter. The herb's key therapeutic compound, glycyrrhizin exerts numerous beneficial effects on the body, making licorice a valuable herb for treating a host of ailments. As a traditional medicine, licorice root has been used for gastric and duodenal ulcers, sore throat, malaria, abdominal pain, insomnia, tuberculosis, sores, abcesses, food poisoning and cancer. Licorice extract has the skin soothing properties and improves the look of an uneven skin tone. Licorice contains glabridin, which is potent anti-oxidant and skin soothing ingredient. One study showed antimicrobial activity against *Staphylococcus aureus*, which can cause skin infections, such as impetigo, cellulitis, and folliculitis. In this study, the researchers used extracts from the leaves and roots of the licorice. Consistent application of skincare that contains licorice root extract can keep your skin moisturized. The presence of "licochalcone" is ideal for individuals with oily skin because licochalcone has shown to control oil content on the skin. Because of these calming properties, licorice root is often incorporated in serum. Licorice root extract is a common ingredient used in many skincare products to lighten the discoloration or pigmentation. Glabridin, an active ingredient in Licorice root, has shown to possesses anti-inflammatory effects and inhibits tyrosinase, a key enzyme that is responsible for making the pigmentation. Liquiritin is another active ingredient, which does not inhibit tyrosinase, but it helps to disperse and remove melanin and pigments in the skin. New basic research shows that licochalcone A, molecule present in licorice root, can suppress cyclooxygenase (COX)-2 and prostaglandin E2 (PGE2) expression after intense sun exposure. Both COX2 and PGE2 are inflammatory enzymes that play a role in triggering an inflammatory reaction and responsible for the painful sensation associated with sunburn. The syrup-like juice from the root contains beneficial plant sterols that increase skin elasticity and fight inflammation and wrinkles. Enzyme hydrolases such as lipases, proteases (chymotrypsin, subtilisin, thermolysin, and papain), esterase use water as a substrate for the reaction to get licorice root extract. It is proved that water, glycerine and enzymes extractions give maximum yield as compared to alcoholic or tincture extracts. Besides alcohol denature the useful constituents of plants.

Skin Care Benefits of Aloe Vera

Aloe Vera truly is a nature's gift and is a popular medicinal plant that has been used for thousands of years in the cosmetic, pharmaceutical and food industries. Its leaves are full of a gel-like substance that contains numerous beneficial compounds. Aloe Vera has a unique, instantly-recognisable smell that transports the senses to a calm place. Aloe Vera is most commonly used as a topical natural product, rubbed onto the skin rather than eaten. Aloe Vera also has many qualities that can aid both our haircare and skincare regimes. Small chain Polysaccharide units (less than 500 Daltons) of Aloe Vera products show maximum absorption and thus maximum benefits.

Aloe Vera is best known for treating skin injuries, but also has several other beneficial effects on health.Aloe Vera contains various powerful antioxidant compounds. Some of these compounds can help inhibit the growth of harmful bacteria particularly causing serious skin and scalp infections. Aloe Vera has long been known as a treatment for sores, particularly burns, including sunburns. A review of 4 experimental studies found that Aloe Vera could reduce the healing time of burns by around 9 days compared to conventional medication. In fact, the FDA first approved Aloe Vera ointment as an over-the-counter medication for skin burns back in 1959. Studies suggest that it is an effective topical treatment for *first- and second-degree burns. There is some preliminary evidence that topical Aloe Vera gel can slow aging of the skin. In one study of 30 women over the age of 45, topical application of the gel was shown to increase collagen production and improve skin elasticity over a 90-day period. Aloe Vera also has the effect of whitening the skin and glow your skin. Some evidences show that Aloe Vera can treat skin conditions like psoriasis, seborrhoea, dandruff, minor burns and skin abrasions, as well as radiation-induced skin injuries and radiation dermatitis. Aloe Vera gel also seems helpful in treating the sores caused by genital herpes in men. Research has shown the Aloe Vera extract can improve the skin's ability to rehydrate itself. Using Aloe Vera-based products can soften the skin without clogging your pores as, unlike some moisturisers, it doesn't leave behind a greasy layer of film after use. It replenishes the moisture loss in the skin, restore the function of the gelatin protein, prevent facial wrinkles, and keep the skin soft, smooth, and elastic. It's long been suggested that Aloe Vera can quicken the skin cell reproduction process. In turn, this can help to fight inflammation and tackle red skin. So, it is a natural treatment for acne scars or stretch marks and reduces blemishes as well as soothes the irritated skin. It has been found that Aloe Vera by cleansing the hair follicles and removing unwanted sebum and residue, rejuvenate your hairs and leave them looking healthier, shinier and softer. This means that when applied to the scalp, you may well see that after your scalp has been cleansed and your roots are nourished by Aloe Vera's goodness, making it a lot more likely that you'll find hair loss and hair breakage slow right down. Aloe Vera is full of all the things that deliver vitality to your hair. Namely vitamins A, C and E - all three of which are key contributors to the healthy cell growth necessary to encourage shiny hair. Aloe Vera is high in collagen which gives it cooling properties that many believe work well to repair sun-damaged hair. Aloe Vera is a fantastic natural product that can reduce the itching and inflammation associated with dandruff and dry scalp. This is due to its antifungal and antibacterial action. Aloe Vera massage on the scalp promote blood circulation of the scalp and stimulate hair growth. At the same time, it can enhance the elasticity of the hair and prevent hair from breaking.

Aloe Vera contains **Vitamins C, E, B-12, folic acid, enzymes, fatty acids and choline content** that may help nourish and strengthen hair.

Hair care professionals recommend Aloe Vera for every type of hair like oily hair, brittle, dry, or damaged hair, curly hair as well as natural hair. African-American hair tends to be very dry, and dermatologists recommend the use of products with natural ingredients, such as Aloe Vera, for hair care.

Blends of Anti-aging Extracts

Exposure to Ultraviolet radiations accelerates skin aging which eventually culminates in wrinkles, laxity, dyspigmentation, roughness and dryness. Aging is a natural process that continues over time. There are two types of aging, that's premature and natural aging. Premature aging is due to bad habits, sun exposure, smoking, frequent alcohol consumption, stress, etc. While natural aging is process that runs out at any time with age. We can`t certainly be stopped, but the fact that we can slow down the aging process by adopting a good lifestyle through the use of natural things that can be obtained from the different types of herbs / plants / trees and chemical products of natural origin in shape of cosmetic medicines. As we get older, dynamic changes find constants that occur in both elastin and collagen[1], making them thick and loose and become deficient in body with time. And that will lead to wrinkles and slackness. Though many active synthetic topicals have been used since years, the present era of treating an aged skin has been diverted towards natural biomaterials as these synthetic topicals pose health and safety risk on human health. Natural extracts, work in two ways, either they stop the destruction of elastin and collagen or they help in the increased production of both essential skin care proteins. The aging of the skin is also associated with the loss of moisture of the skin. Hyaluronic acid besides elastin and collagen is a natural component of the skin and maintains the elasticity and firmness of the skin.

BLEND OF ALOE VERA, DILL SEED, SAFFRON, CASHEW NUTS, NEETLE AND GREEN COFFEE BEANS

Blend of anti-aging extracts exert more benefits as compared to extracts taken individually. But care should be taken while selecting different ingredients to boost anti-aging effect. Because in some cases when different ingredients are mixed together then they may chemically interact with each other (due to chemical instability) and antagonize the effect of other and that can pose harmful effects rather than benefits.

When Aloe Vera, Dill Seed, Saffron, Cashew Nuts, Nettle and Green Coffee Beans are combined together through extraction process, (usually carried out through water and glycerine and or enzyme assisted extraction) exert a powerful anti-aging effect. This greater effectiveness of blend is due to the combined anti-aging indications of these extracts.

CHIEF INGREDIENRS OF THIS BLEND

Main ingredients of this blend include,

- Aloe-Vera
- Dill seed
- Saffron
- Cashew Nuts.
- Nettle.
- Green coffee beans.
- Water
- Glycerine
- Enzymes
- Others, like natural fragrance, gelling agents, colouring agents and flavouring agents etc. (These ingredients are optional).

INDICATIONS OF THIS BLEND

This blend of herbs contains vitamins, amino acids, minerals, peptides etc that stimulates youthful skin with a variety of other benefits for their rejuvenating powers. It combats wrinkles, fine lines and leaves your skin feeling soft, silky and more elastic. This blend can be the necessary element for your routine skin care regimes. This blend is particularly indicated for dehydrated skin, signs of aging, wrinkles, tired skin and for nourishing hair and scalp.

ALOE VERA contains various powerful antioxidant compounds. Some of these compounds can help inhibit the growth of harmful bacteria particularly causing serious skin and scalp infections. Aloe Vera has long been known as a treatment for sores, particularly burns, including sunburns. There is some preliminary evidence that topical Aloe Vera gel can slow aging of the skin. In one study of 30 women over the age of 45, topical application of the gel was shown to increase collagen production and improve skin elasticity over a 90-day period. Aloe Vera also has the effect of whitening the skin and glow your skin. Some evidences show that Aloe Vera can treat skin conditions like psoriasis, seborrhoea, dandruff, minor burns and skin abrasions, as well as radiation-induced skin injuries and radiation dermatitis[4]. Aloe Vera gel also seems helpful in treating the sores caused by genital herpes in men. It's long been suggested that Aloe Vera can quicken the skin cell reproduction process. In turn, this can help to fight inflammation and tackle red skin. So, it is a natural treatment for acne scars or stretch marks and reduces blemishes as well as soothes the irritated skin. It has been found that Aloe Vera by cleansing the hair follicles and removing unwanted sebum[6] and residue, rejuvenate your hairs and leave them looking healthier, shinier and softer.

DILL SEED extract has the capability to protect the skin and slow down the aging process thereby producing vital skin proteins like elastin and or collagen. Dill seed extract stimulates elastin and collagen synthesis by activating dermal fibroblasts. Dill seed extract also increases the production of the precursor of elastin, tropo-elastin. Dill extract helps increase expression of enzymes in skin that generates elastin and help rebuild skin's structural integrity. Several scientific studies have shown that topical application of formulas with dill may help to reinforce skin elasticity and firmness, thus improving the overall appearance of skin. As a result, the benefits of dill extract are often infused in anti-aging skincare formulas. Due to the anti-microbial activity, dill destroy the micro-organism and thus prevents the destruction of beauty proteins.

SAFFRON has antibacterial and antiseptic properties, and as a result can fight off acne and pimples, thereby providing for a youthful glowing skin. Saffron not only clears acne scars and inflammation, but also minimizes the oil secreted by the sebaceous glands. Saffron is a good exfoliating agent and therefore can help remove signs of aging on the skin. Saffron when combined with other ingredients is very effective against wrinkles and fine lines. Saffron is very effective against pigmentation[7] and tanning[8]. Saffron contains many vitamins and antioxidants and also serves as an anti-inflammatory which soothes skin and can prevent breakouts.

CASHEW NUTS do better for your skin, hair, and body than you can imagine. Cashews are rich in antioxidants that promote the growth of new cells in your skin. This enables your skin to regenerate faster and helps maintain the elasticity. Eating cashews daily can also help your body to fight against free radicals.

Cashews are the storehouse of zinc, magnesium, selenium, iron, and phosphorus. These nuts are also rich in proteins and vitamins that can improve the skin's complexion and prevents wrinkle.

The Cashew nuts contain copper which promoted hair growth and prevents your mane from premature greying. Cashews also make your tresses smooth and silky. Cashews are packed with potassium and other essential nutrients that prevent your scalp from shedding hair unnecessarily and promotes hair growth. This nut contains high amount of vitamin C which can reduce blemishes and tans. Vitamin C also slows down the process of weight gain, which in turn lowers the chances of stretch marks.

NETTLE is high in phenols, which give nettle powerful antioxidant properties and help keep the free radicals under control when used in skincare. Research has also found high anti-microbial activity in nettle extracts (Gülçin, 2004). Dr. Joseph Buller describes replacing the use of liquor arsenicals (essentially a poisonous 'medicine' used in the 1800s to 'cure' all sorts of ailments) with nettle decoction or extract. Virtually all his patients were cured of their chronic skin diseases. Nettle extract is also used in the treatment of scalp problems and incorporated into a variety of hair products. Nettle roots are used to relieve eczema and dandruff and are reputed to stimulate hair growth.

GREEN COFFEE BEANS contain two major constituents that's Chlorogenic acid and Caffeine. So, the health benefits are because of these constituents. Green bean coffee extract holds many antioxidant properties, the majority of which have been shown to slow the effects of aging. The high concentration of chlorogenic acid present in the green coffee extract reduces redness associated with excessive sunlight exposure. Caffeine also contains anti-aging properties. It limits photodamage, decreases skin roughness and wrinkle formation, and reduces the appearance of crow's feet. No wonder dermatologists and skincare companies include green coffee bean extract in their products

<u>References</u>

- Zhang C, Lu Y, Tao L, Tao X, Su X, Wei D. Tyrosinase inhibitory effects and inhibition mechanisms of nobiletin and hesperidin from citrus peel crude extracts. J Enzyme Inhib Med Chem. 2007 Feb;22(1):83-90.

- Guardia T, Rotelli AE, Juarez AO, Pelzer LE. Anti-inflammatory properties of plant flavonoids. Effects of rutin, quercetin and hesperidin on adjuvant arthritis in rat. Farmaco. 2001 Sep;56(9):683-7.

- Snyder SM, Reber JD, Freeman BL, Orgad K, Eggett DL, Parker TL. Controlling for sugar and ascorbic acid, a mixture of flavonoids matching navel oranges significantly increases human postprandial serum antioxidant capacity. Nutr Res. 2011 Jul;31(7):519-26.

- <u>Buller, J. 1854. *The use of an extract and decoction of the common stinging nettle in some chronic skin diseases.* Assoc Med J. 1854 November 10; 2(97): 1010–1012.</u>

- <u>Gülçin, I., Küfrevio O.I., Oktay, M., Büyükokuro, M.E. 2004. *Antioxidant, antimicrobial, antiulcer and analgesic*</u>

- *activities of nettle (Urtica dioica L.).* Journal of Ethnopharmacology 90 (2004) 205–215.
- https://kcallife.com/wellness/a120/
- https://nutritiondata.self.com/facts/vegetables-and-vegetable-products/2626/2
- https://www.ncbi.nlm.nih.gov/pubmed/25361771/
- https://www.ncbi.nlm.nih.gov/pubmed/21914489
- https://www.stylecraze.com/articles/benefits-of-spinach-for-skin-hair-and-health/#gref
- https://www.ncbi.nlm.nih.gov/pubmed/27445214
- https://www.ncbi.nlm.nih.gov/pubmed/22809031
- https://www.ncbi.nlm.nih.gov/pmc/articles/PMC2720939/
- https://www.ncbi.nlm.nih.gov/pubmed/21785631
- http://www.ibiol.ro/plant/volume%2055/art03.pdf
- https://www.healthline.com/health/alfalfa-for-hair#takeaway
- https://www.aveenomd.com/our-ingredients/feverfew
- Sharma VK, Sethuraman G. Parthenium dermatitis. Dermatitis. 2007 Dec;18(4):183-90.
- https://practicaldermatology.com/articles/2010-oct/applications-of-popular-botanical-ingredients-in-otc-skincare
- https://lilyfarmfreshskincare.com/how-feverfew-helps-skin/
- https://www.stylecraze.com/articles/benefits-of-marshmallow-root/#gref
- https://www.ncbi.nlm.nih.gov/pubmed/19799989
- https://www.ncbi.nlm.nih.gov/pmc/articles/PMC4418059/
- https://www.newdirectionsaromatics.com/blog/products/all-about-evening-primrose-oil.html
- https://www.besthealthmag.ca/best-looks/beauty/evening-primrose-oil-benefits/
- https://www.verywellhealth.com/the-benefits-of-evening-primrose-oil-89561
- https://www.ncbi.nlm.nih.gov/pubmed/20807260

- https://www.ncbi.nlm.nih.gov/pmc/articles/PMC3569896/
- Sohm B, Cenizo V, André V, Zahouani H, Pailler-Mattei C, Vogelgesang B. Evaluation of the efficacy of a dill extract *in vitro* and *in vivo*. *International Journal of Cosmetic Science*. 2011;33(2):157–163. [PubMed]
- https://www.peacefuldumpling.com/natural-beauty-dill-seed-oil-improved-elastin
- https://onlinelibrary.wiley.com/doi/full/10.1111/j.1600-0625.2009.00862.x
- https://www.ncbi.nlm.nih.gov/pubmed/19469891
- https://somayurvedic.com/products/anti-aging-cream
- https://chiltanpure.com/product/aloe-vera-gel/
- https://chiltanpure.com/product/cocktail-essential-oil/
- http://extranewsbuzz.us/2019/08/27/7-japanese-anti-aging-secrets/
- http://ijpsr.com/bft-article/studies-on-an-anti-aging-formulation-prepared-using-aloe-vera-blended-collagen-and-chitosan/?view=fulltext
- https://www.goldensaffron.com/blog/health/amazing-benefits-of-saffron-on-skin
- https://www.medicalnewstoday.com/articles/318591.php#-improves-the-skin-
- https://www.webmd.com/diet/supplement-guide-aloe-vera#1
- https://www.ncbi.nlm.nih.gov/pubmed/20807260
- https://www.ncbi.nlm.nih.gov/pmc/articles/PMC3569896/

- Sohm B, Cenizo V, André V, Zahouani H, Pailler-Mattei C, Vogelgesang B. Evaluation of the efficacy of a dill extract *in vitro* and *in vivo*. *International Journal of Cosmetic Science*. 2011;33(2):157–163. [PubMed]

- https://www.peacefuldumpling.com/natural-beauty-dill-seed-oil-improved-elastin

- https://onlinelibrary.wiley.com/doi/full/10.1111/j.1600-0625.2009.00862.x

- https://www.ncbi.nlm.nih.gov/pubmed/19469891

- Buller, J. 1854. *The use of an extract and decoction of the common stinging nettle in some chronic skin diseases.* Assoc Med J. 1854 November 10; 2(97): 1010–1012.

- Gülçin, I., Küfrevio O.I., Oktay, M., Büyükokuro, M.E. 2004. *Antioxidant, antimicrobial, antiulcer and analgesic activities of nettle (Urtica dioica L.).* Journal of Ethnopharmacology 90 (2004) 205–215.

- https://www.herzindagi.com/diet-nutrition/amazing-benefits-of-cashew-nuts-for-skin-hair-eyes-article-131000

- https://food.ndtv.com/food-drinks/7-incredible-cashew-nut-benefits-from-heart-health-to-gorgeous-hair-1415221

- https://www.superfoodly.com/health-benefits-of-cashews/

- https://www.ora.organic/blogs/news/the-benefits-of-green-coffee-bean

www.ingramcontent.com/pod-product-compliance
Lightning Source LLC
Chambersburg PA
CBHW021409160726
47994CB00007B/3138